CONVERSATION PATTERNS
FOR SOFTWARE PROFESSIONALS

Michał Bartyzel

Conversation Patterns for Software Professionals

Published by C4Media, publisher of InfoQ.com.

Production Editor: Ana Ciobotaru
Copy Editor: Lawrence Nyveen
Interior Design: Dragos Balasoiu

ISBN 978-1-365-41048-2

To my family: Edyta, Nadia, and Adam.

Contents

Acknowledgements

Most of all, the greatest thanks belongs to the editors of InfoQ, with whom I had the pleasure to cooperate: Shane Hastie, Roxana Bacila, and Ana Ciobotaru. Thanks to you, this book finally will appear in English – I have been waiting for this opportunity impatiently.

Second, I would like to thank the teams I have collaborated with and the participants I have trained. They were the first users of the methods described in this book.

If you think that the business you are dealing with does not know what it wants, you are in the right place. In this short book, you will learn how to work with the business people. You will learn how to manage a conversation, explore needs, and clarify expectations.

Here we go!

Michał Bartyzel

PART
ONE

Between
the business
and IT

Hello! Thank you for having decided to devote your time to reading this book. Since we are going to spend a few hours together, I suggest that we call each other by name. My name is Michał (at least, in Polish).

It might surprise you that I wrote this chapter last. Now that all ideas have gained their real shape, I know that in this book you will find a practical guide to collecting requirements and conducting a conversation with the client. I secretly hope that at some stage you will come back here to confront my presented methods of action with your own experiences. If you want to share your thoughts on the effectiveness of these techniques, you have a question, or a new idea comes to your mind, e-mail me at m.bartyzel@bnsit.pl.

Who is this book for?

This book is set in the context of the process of software development. I am a member and supporter of agile processes[1] so first and foremost I address this book to the members of agile teams. I am convinced that it will help you respond to the Agile Manifesto's[2] calls more fully.

Whether the software is produced in an agile way or not, the process of working on it involves, among others, the following activities:

- collecting and analyzing business requirements,
- collecting and analyzing user requirements and functionalities,
- designing the system architecture,
- programming,
- testing,
- implementation, and
- maintenance such as fixing bugs, adding new functionalities, etc.

Almost all of these points entails an action that can be called "collecting requirements". Collecting requirements will mean *discovering what the client expects from the IT system*. One of the key components of this process of discovery is a conversation or an interview with the client and the users. Depending on the approach, the people contacting the client/user may

---

1 http://c2.com/cgi/wiki?AgileProcesses
2 http://www.agilemanifesto.org

be developers, senior developers, business analysts, system analysts, functional analysts, designers, and architects.[3]

This book is for all of them.

How much management is there in requirements management?

Do you remember your last conversation with a client about software being developed? Did you notice that as the conversation progressed, you started to understand each other better? The actual needs of the client became clearer to you. Perhaps you used slogans or symbols to write down some information on a sheet of paper. These concise notes were enough to appeal to your common understanding of the subject of your conversation. This common understanding is called "shared context of conversation".

Figure 1.1. Shared context of conversation.

Everything works fine as long as remains between you and that same person. But what will you do if you have to introduce someone else to the subject? You usually either take time to reconstruct the shared context in a new discussion or you prepare a document.

The problem with the document is that it is only the final form of the findings of the conversation. It does not reflect the process of inventing solutions – it only presents their final shape. It contains no associations or circumstances that led the author to these and not those applications. For this reason, a person left alone with the document may not understand it as well as you do.

---

3   These roles might have different names in different organizations.

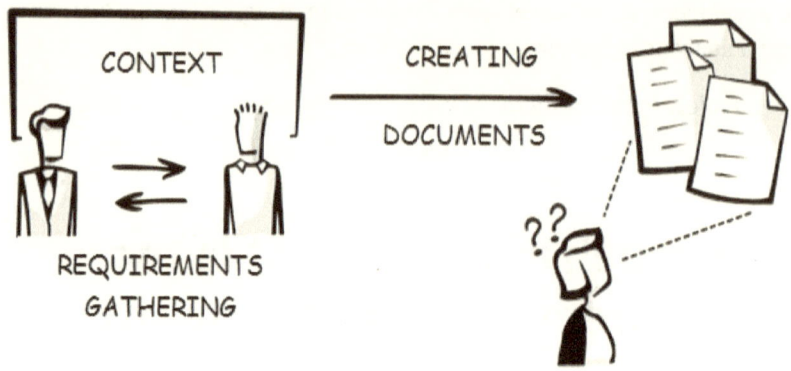

Figure 1.2. Creating the document.

Documenting requirements is very important, but to document them, you must first collect them.

Many publications that have "requirements management" in their titles devote a lot of space to classification of requirements, documenting requirements, and UML[4] diagrams. But what about "management"? Requirements management is a process that should let you answer the following questions:

- How do new requirements influence the existing system?
- What should be changed in the system as a consequence of the new requirements?
- How to manage the implementation of new requirements?

One of the most painful phenomena in the process of software development is the change of requirements. The essence of requirements management is controlling changes, implementing them, and monitoring their impact on a system that is already running.

In order to appropriately manage requirements, we have to reach the essence of the client's needs and constantly analyze them. As long as the system is used, the process of requirements management must continue, because it has to constantly adapt to the changing reality. Similarly, as long as the requirements management functions, you have to know how to collect the requirements, specify them, and reach their motivation to efficiently complete your tasks.

---

4 Unified Modeling Language.

A client who does not know what he wants

Doesn't it bother you why the clients are often thought to not know what they want from the developers, analysts, project leaders, and testers? On the other hand, why is it obvious that the IT people always know what they want from the clients? It happens that we are strongly attached to such opinions, especially if we have formed them during a series of meetings with non-technical people. Nevertheless, I think you will agree that this one-sided view is not entirely fair. Considering the two parties of communication will expand your perspective.

When you sit in front of the client and you do not know what he or she is trying to convey, you should realize that this person has a need and believes that information technology will definitely help with this need. If a client did not need something, he or she wouldn't set an appointment with you. For this reason, I am asking you to adopt the following assumptions in the course of reading this book:

- **The clients always know what they want** – they know that they want to solve a problem, to achieve a goal, to improve something.
- **The clients do not always know what they need** – because they are focused mostly on their business processes.
- **The clients often do not realize the consequences of their expectations** – because they are experts in their business activities and not in information technology.

If you agree to think this way for a moment, we will look for tools that will help you work with business clients.

Have you ever wondered what it would be like if you woke up one day to find that – not without surprise – all your knowledge of IT, of programming, and of the systems was gone? All that knowledge and experience that you had gathered with so much effort – disappeared. Your entire ability to work with a computer has come down to pressing the power and the reset buttons. What would it be like to experience something like that?

Adopting this perspective, please explain to me that you would like me to create software that will be your personal schedule. Describe your expectations for this application. Is this an easy task or a difficult one? What kind of things will you say from this IT-agnostic point of view?

Probably you will talk about:

- your ideas,
- things you have seen in similar applications,
- things that someone told you about such applications,
- your problems with paper schedules, and
- your worries about using an electronic schedule instead of a paper one.

Although most clients are probably much more educated in terms of computers, this short experiment allows you to look at the world through the eyes of a stereotypical client. How would you feel if I told you that you do not know what you want? You would surely think that I am wrong as, after all, you know what you want: you want to have an electronic organizer and you are trying to explain it as best you can.

Now, let's come back to the developer's perspective. If you are given a task to implement – say, "create an electronic schedule" – you would like to learn more about that. What should it look like? What functionalities should it make available? How should it exactly work? This is the crux of the matter. To create software, you need specific and detailed information that the client has not delivered to you. Why? Because he does not know that he should. He describes his expectations as best he can. It is surprising for him that you would like to know whether the notes should be permanently stored and for how long, how many people should have access to the schedule, and if the schedule is to be used on a PC, a notebook, a tablet, or a phone. The answers to some of these questions are obvious to the client. Should notes be kept? *Yes, of course!* How long? *Forever!* Other questions might surprise the client because he does not realize that such things are important in the process of creating software. Asking questions remains the best way to learn the thoughts of others – at least until we master telepathy.

The situations described here happen every day. In hundreds of companies, in thousands of meetings, millions of frustrated participants repeatedly ask the same questions: *What is he saying? Why does not he listen to me? What does he mean? Why does not he understand?* When you talk with someone, at least fifty percent of effective communication depends on you.

In a moment, you will learn how to make the most of this.

PART TWO

What does it mean to "think in a business way"?

In the world of business people, one of the most frequently repeated objections towards the developers is "developers do not think in a business way." But what this "business thinking" means is not entirely clear. Does it mean thinking about benefits, money, users, or perhaps sales? Or maybe something else? Let me take a closer look at this.

The nonchalance of developers

A small coincidence once shed some light on "business thinking" for me.

I was made product owner in a project whose aim was to create a website that provided video-on-demand (VOD) services. Together with the sponsor, I worked out the substantive terms, and prepared user screens and specified the flow between them. I could see the shape of the product – on paper, but still…. We also listed many new opportunities for the product to monetize. Once we fairly accurately knew what we wanted, we engaged the developers.

After several iterations, the time came to present the results. I was waiting impatiently for the webpage to load... and when it did, I suddenly turned pale. What I saw in no way resembled my ideas. Nor was there much that looked like screen layouts that I had been drawing so meticulously. When the developers were presenting the product, they would constantly repeat, "It's going to change," "Here you only need to change the skin," "It actually works." I could not believe that they considered their task finished despite the clearly defined – and unmet – expectations. It occurred to me then that the developers that I worked with considered the task complete when they had a well-considered and implemented mechanism of action (i.e. the back end) and some effects on the side of the user interface. To me, that was unacceptable. Although I had worked a lot as a developer, at that time I really understood what the people from the business feel when they get not what they expected.

There was one phenomenon that particularly caught my attention – I called it the nonchalance of developers. This nonchalance is characterized by not paying attention to the terms that are important for the business. I made a short note in which I listed the names that I used in conversations with the developers to define the user stories and the names that I had ultimately seen on the screens of the presented application.

Name that I used	Name used by the developers
My cinematheque	List of films
Add a series	Add a category
Add an episode	Add an FLV file
Paid/unpaid	Status [checkbox]
Labels	Tag cloud
Duration: 0 h 35 mins	Length: 2100000 ms
House M.D. Season 1 episode 19	87a1b230ff910912.flv

Table 2.1. Names wanted by the business and names used by the developers.

It turns out that despite the conversations and information provided, the developers and I thought differently about the same business reality. I thought to use terms that came from other VOD sites. The developers, in turn, saw some very specific components of the graphical interface in what I was telling them and what I drawing. They saw lists, checkboxes, menus, buttons – they thought programmatically.

Words and their meaning

Does it really matter how we think and what names we use? Isn't it enough that the system has been created and it is working? Of course, the most important aspect is that the system is up and running, but the costs incurred to achieve future work will also be important. (I am talking about the costs of collaboration between the business and IT).

Take a look at Figure 2.1. If you call something a "film", there is a specific meaning associated with this name: a film is a kind of a spectacle composed of moving images. If you use the word "film" in this sense, it becomes obvious that the film can be viewed, borrowed, bought, recorded, etc. In other words, you assume that this name entails a set of rules that describes how the term "film" can be used and how the physical object that is a "film" relates to other objects. For example, a TV series is a film, a film may consist of episodes, etc. This set of rules, whose existence you assume, could be called the "algebra of business names" because it deals with the rules that govern the names used in a given field of business.

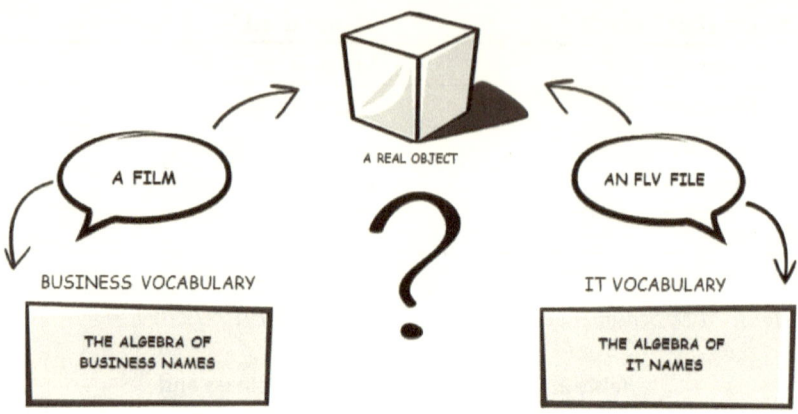

Figure 2.1. Words have their meaning.

However, if you call the same physical object a "FLV file", you automatically associate a somewhat different meaning with it and you think of totally different rules that govern this name, because an FLV file can be streamed, encrypted, copied, saved as read-only, linked, etc. You cannot do any of these things with a "film"; you are referring to the term "FLV file".

This is where the main problem lies. The business uses words from the dictionary of business and these words have specific meaning in the field of business. Using these words, the business operates in the algebra of business names. On the other hand, when the developers look at the same physical thing, they use the names taken from the dictionary of the developers and from the field of programming. The developers use names governed by completely different rules than those of the business. They are governed by the principles of the algebra of IT names.

Business terms exist in context

In my earlier discussion, I used the colloquial term "word". Let me clarify. When you talk with the client about the business, you discover business terms that have specific meaning within the area under discussion. As shown in Figure 2.2, a business term consists of: a name that you immediately discover in the course of the conversation – for example, a "film" or a "training module"; a meaning that is a particular aspect of the business reality entailed by a given name; and a rule, a principle forming the aforementioned algebra of business names.

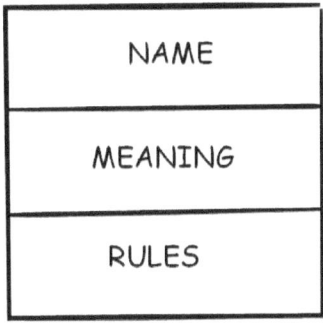

Figure 2.2. The structure of a business term.

A crucial issue to recognize is that in the course of a conversation the business terms are always used in a given context. The context is all that is known when you have a conversation with the client. This "all that is known" can be the knowledge and experience of your interlocutor, the information contained in the documentation, all the design objectives, external regulations (e.g. legal regulations), etc.

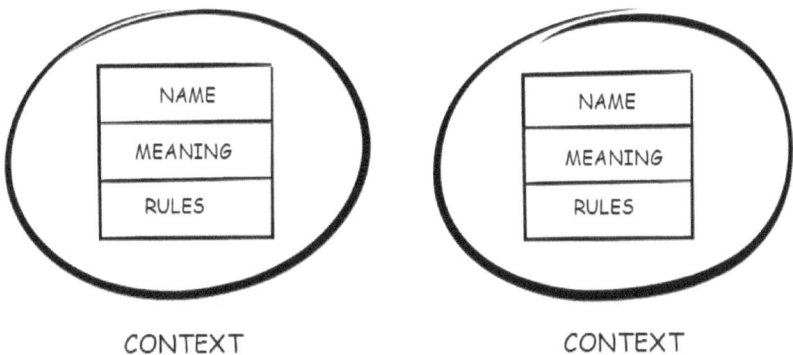

Figure 2.3. A business term exists in context.

The most charming feature of the context is that while its component information is known, it is not explicitly stated. This means that the interlocutor assumes that you know the context and gives you information in relation to that context. To balance this, you certainly follow a similar pattern of behavior. ☺ Misunderstandings related to context are well illustrated by the aforementioned example with the term of "film". The same term has been used in two different contexts – once in the technical context of data storage and once in the business context of an artistic spectacle. Within different contexts, the same term takes on different meanings and implicitly entails different sets of rules for forming different algebras. At this point, we discover a precise and useful definition of context: a named area of a given field of business in which each individual business term has exactly one meaning.[1]

The example with the term "film" is obvious because the difference in contexts is very clear. In the section on how to make requirements more detailed, you will find examples that are not so clear and some techniques for identifying and naming the context. There, you will also learn how to use it to collect requirements in an efficient way.

To think in a business way

It is time to demystify the mysterious term "business thinking".

To think in a business way is nothing else than to use names and meanings that come from the dictionary of the business, and to use them only to the extent permitted by the rules of the algebra of the business names.

Summary

This chapter was devoted to the explanation of how words build expectations. There are meanings hidden behind names, and names entail rules that we use to think about what the names actually described. Context is important to a conversation because it is the context that determines the meaning and the rules related to the names used in the course of the conversation.

One of the main difficulties in the process of collecting requirements is the fact that the dictionary of terms used by the business is quite different from the dictionary of terms used by IT. Business thinking, which is the understanding of client needs, is first of all the ability to understand how the clients think and how they describe the work they are doing.

---

1   Eric Evans coined this definition of context as "bounded context" by in his book *Domain-Driven Design*.

PART
THREE

The art of
asking questions

In this chapter, you will learn the most important things on how to effectively lead a conversation with the client. I'll talk about leading a conversation, adopting the client's perspective and the most common mistakes.

Who leads the conversation?

The person who says more? The one who speaks louder? Or the one who is able to quickly and effectively convince others to invest in his/her ideas?

The person who actually leads the conversation and manages its direction is the one who asks questions! Asking the right questions leads a conversation in a controlled manner and makes the most of it in terms of collecting requirements.

I once got a call from a consultant who represented a mobile telephony provider. As he began to present the company's offer, I turned on a stopwatch. The consultant spoke without interruption for almost 10 minutes. He did not ask me even a single question. Of course, I soon stopped listening to him, and he finally heard me shouting a short "No!"

Questions mark the border between a conversation and a monologue. If you don't ask questions, you will never know what your client really needs.

To take the initiative in a conversation means to focus on asking well-considered questions and to listen to the answers.

What does it mean to look from the client's perspective?

Some time ago, I had car accident. Luckily, only the car suffered. My last stage of post-accident proceedings was to enforce the payment of the compensation from the insurer. My exchange of e-mails with the consultant representing the lessor proceeded as follows:

E-mail 1: Me to the consultant

Good morning,

I would like to finish the case of the car. What are the next steps?

//

E-mail 2: The Consultant to me

Hello,

After receiving payments from the insurance company, the contract will be transferred for settlement. Once the note has been entered in the accounts by the accounting department, a settlement document will be sent to the lessee by registered mail and with an acknowledgement of receipt.

E-mail 3: Me to the consultant

Dear Katarzyna,

Thank you your reply. If possible, please let me clarify my questions:

When the insurance company pays, when will I get the money?

What should be done and when should I do it in order for the money to be paid quickly and without delays?

//

E-mail 4: The consultant to me

Dear Michał,

As I wrote in my previous e-mail, the contract will be forwarded for settlement upon the receipt of money from the supplements.

It takes up to 10 days for the accounting department to enter the note in the accounts and settle the payment.

The document is sent by registered mail and if the settlement includes an amount to be refunded, in order to get a refund, it is necessary to send a request signed by the representatives of the company, where you specify the bank account number.

In order to accomplish this, you will need to return a corrective invoice that you were provided with.

//

E-mail 5: Me to the consultant

Dear Katarzyna,

Thank you for a detailed explanation of the upcoming steps. One thing is unclear for me, and this is actually the most important issue from my previous e-mail: when exactly will I get the money?

//

E-mail 6: The consultant to me

Dear Michał,

I think it will take up to 30 days.

What would you call what happened during this conversation? What did I ask about – and what did the consultant talk about? Answer these questions, and listen to another story....

> *My wife asked me to fix the handle on our bedroom door. The problem was that the handle was creaking and our daughter would wake up whenever any of us opened the door to our bedroom.*
>
> *I dismantled the handle and I covered every suspicious part if its mechanism with grease. Since I had just got back from a training conducted for one of our clients, I immediately decided that I had the chance to apply the best standards known to me in this work: I decided to formulate clear acceptance criteria.*
>
> *"Listen," I turned to my wife. "How many times do you have to press the handle and have it not creak to convince yourself that it has been completely repaired?"*
>
> *My wife looked at me in astonishment and after a moment she said, "The handle will be repaired when Nadia does not wake up when I leave the room."*

What would you call what happened in that dialogue? What kind of acceptance criteria did I formulate – and what did my wife expect? What does this second story have in common with the first? Before you fully answer these questions, listen to a yet another....

We prepared a product demo for our client. We were thrilled, because the scope of that issue featured an innovative functionality written in one of the newest technologies.

We proudly presented the scenarios of stories and the level of sophistication of the new functionality. When the time for a summary came, the client said, "Listen, this is great! Really! What I like most is that you have done so that I can press control-C in Word, and then control-V in the form – and the text appears."

The team was speechless....

What was the team focused on – and what did the client appreciate? Considering the activity of the people involved, what does this third story have in common with the previous stories?

Whose domain is it?

In the previous chapter, "What does it mean to 'think in a business way'?", I talked a lot about a business domain and using concepts from that domain – in a word, that to "think in a business way" is to think and to communicate with the client according to the rules pertaining to his/her field of business. It is possible that you have gone through the chapter on business thinking quickly because you wanted to get here to learn some specific techniques for collecting requirements. If that indeed was the case, now is your last chance to return and to carefully read it.

Theoretically, talking about the domain, the dictionary, and communication is simple. The chapter on business thinking is also conceptually and technically simple. Nevertheless, the stories presented here are great anti-examples of the lack of understanding of the client's domain and way of thinking.

In the first story, I repeated my questions about the provision of compensation, but the consultant described the business processes that governed my case in the lessor's company. I was interested in a tangible result on my bank account, i.e. the receipt of compensation, while the consultant would tell me about her perspective without any consideration of my perspective.

In the second story, I focused on a technical test – a door handle that creaked. My mistake was not that the test was not automatic; my mistake lay in the fact that my wife was expecting a specific effect in her reality (domain), while I focused on verifying if the solution worked technically.

In the last story, the team was disappointed because the client valued a feature of the operating system, which existed out of the box. At the same time, the client did not pay much attention to the advanced functionalities that we had developed with so much effort. The problem was that this insignificant copy/paste function solved his most common difficulty in using that tool.

These three stories featured the same pattern: the person from the technical side (the lessor's consultant, me, the team) did not enter the domain of client (me, my wife, the client) even for a moment. They might have used the right words, but they completely ignored their meaning, the rules governing these words, and the business context.

To enter the domain of the client is to think like the client to assess whether the solutions are fit for their purpose. It means to almost be the client. Whenever you formulate an expected functionality, an acceptance test, a need, you always need to ask yourself whose functionality it is – yours or your client's? Whose test is it – yours or your client's? Whose need is it – yours or your client's?

When you approach this issue from a purely financial point of view, you can say the following: the clients pay when they see a specific effect in their domain. Whatever you formulate with the client – the stories, the acceptance tests, the criteria, the needs, the problems, the benefits – always enter the domain of the client and formulate each of these things in the context of the client's domain. Otherwise, you will create software for yourself – not for the client. There is no need to mention who will pay for it, right?

Awareness of the vocabulary used in the course of the conversation

In the previous chapter, I also wrote that it is extremely important to communicate using the client's language, which in practice means to use the same terms in the same sense, to know the rules that follow from these terms, and to consider the business context of the client. On the other hand, in the course of the conversation you will certainly miss or fail to understand something or you will comprehend it contrary to the intentions of the interlocutor. This type of interference is unavoidable. Nevertheless, you can minimize the impact of these problems by training your self-awareness during the conversation.

The term "awareness" might seem mysterious and alien, but it actually entails a clearly defined ability to stay aware of the course of a phenomenon that you experience. This means you can talk and work on the awareness of voice, the awareness of hearing, the awareness of movement, or the awareness of emotions (Goleman, 1997).

In our case, what counts is the awareness of the language used by the client and the language used by the person collecting requirements. This awareness enables you to quickly and effectively recognize the vocabulary used by the business and to improve cooperation. Before I define what it is, listen to another story.…

> One of my coaching teachers demonstrated an intriguing ability to memorize the names of the participants during a workshop. After participants introduced themselves, the coach would address each by name until the end of the workshop. When used at the beginning of the training, this simple procedure relaxes the atmosphere. I decided to learn how to do it.
>
> I would repeat this technique of memorizing names[1] during every training and after more than a dozen occasions, I could remember the names of all the participants − whether they changed seating places or not. The training groups I work with consist of six to 18 people. Once, during a larger event, I managed to remember the names of 40 participants for one day.
>
> After a while, I noticed an interesting phenomenon. Sometimes during an introduction, the participant says something that distracts me. This may be an expectation that does not fall within the scope of training, an issue in which I am not competent, or a problem that I have not yet encountered. I noticed that if such a question appears, the thought of it dominates my awareness and makes it very difficult for me to focus on memorizing names. Consequently, rather than all names, I am able to memorize only a few.

---

1 Mnemonic techniques related to memorizing names are presented in the book Pamięć. *Trening interaktywny* [*Memory: Interactive Training*] by Maciej Szurawski, Wydawnictwo AHA, 2007

The story above illustrates awareness during conversation. When I'm focused on memorizing names and I speak with participants on neutral topics, I memorize their names without any problems. But if something strongly distracts my attention, I lose the ability to simultaneously talk with the participants and memorize their names. Therefore, the awareness during a conversation is the ability to simultaneously participate in and observe that conversation.

When your awareness abandons you during a meeting with a client, you almost certainly won't pick up the subtle differences in the vocabulary used. The main reason for losing the thread of a conversation is taking the time to figure out how to fulfill the requirements that you are talking about. This is a very serious mistake! Please, forgive me for using an exclamation point in the previous sentence, but this moment is so important that it deserves even more exclamation points. When you start thinking about how to meet the demands, you stop listening. You are no longer in the here and now; your thoughts begin to drift to the future. Instead of discovering the requirements, you focus on meeting them.

When a typical client talks with a typical specialist about some typical requirements for a typical system, their thinking processes run quite differently, as shown in table 3.1.

Talking about the requirements, the client thinks about...	Talking about the requirements, the specialist thinks about...
<ul><li>sample situations from their work</li><li>ideas on the expected system</li><li>the UI screens</li><li>the process of using the system</li></ul>	<ul><li>the solutions</li><li>potential technical problems</li><li>the internal structure of the system</li></ul>

Table 3.1. Differences in the client's and the specialist's ways of thinking in the course of a conversation about requirements.

As you can see, the business interlocutor has something like a slideshow in his head. The slides that follow are the screens of the system and some ideas on how this system might work. The technical specialist, in turn, thinks about the solutions, focusing on the internal structure of the system and its mechanics. The specialist focuses on what to change, to add, or to improve.

You probably guess that moving from one slide to another takes very little time. On the other hand, upgrading solutions developed in your head lasts far longer. If, in the course of the conversation, you devote most of your attention to the solutions and the other person "changes the slide" two or three times, you will lose the thread.

During a conversation, the client also invents and verifies the requirements, so these requirements will vary. If you focus on solutions at this stage, you do unnecessary work. Why wonder about the detailed execution of something that might change many times before you even start the development work?

Summary

In this chapter, I talked about two important skills underlying effective conversations. These are the ability to adopt the perspective of the client and the ability to lead a conversation in a conscious way.

PART
FOUR

What is a business need?

Consider which answer to one of the following questions – before reading this chapter – will help you make the most out of its practical content:

- What will this chapter be about?
- What was the most difficult part of my recent conversation with the client?
- Why do I repeat the same mistakes when talking to the client?
- What new opportunities would arise if my conversations with clients went the way I want them to go?

Which question did you pick? If you are not quite sure, I encourage you to go ahead and read this chapter. We'll return to these questions a bit later.

Any software is created for someone: a person that will pay for it or a person that will use it. The main purpose of software is to improve someone else's work. Although, formally, all the people that will be affected by it are called "stakeholders", software development teams frequently call these people "the business people" or an even a shorter option: "the business".

What is to be done?

If you want to write appropriate (that is, useful) software, you need to somehow get the information on what to do from the business. The difficulty of doing that lies in the fact that the information you get is diverse. For example, you might hear:

- information about the current state like "The report is not working;"
- an excerpt from a business rule like "If a month has 31 days, I want to receive a notification at the beginning of the next month unless there are holidays, in which case I don't want any notifications;"
- a story like "I once saw similar software with a nice feature that could read amounts from sales receipts on its own;" or
- an idea about functionality like "Let's insert some columns from the previous version and in addition to ID, let's add two columns from the dictionary – in Polish and in Hungarian."

Although from the point of view of your clients, these explanations are hitting the mark, you need a lot more information to create useful software. First of all, you need more detail and concrete goals.

Years of experience in the industry have shown me that the best way to get concrete and detailed knowledge from the business is to structure it. Structuring can be defined as organizing the acquired knowledge according to predetermined criteria, for example: functional requirements, non-functional requirements, domain-specific rules, architecture, and implementation limitations. Such an ordered collection of information is a checklist for those who collect it and it helps them identify what they already know, what else they need to know, and what they have to specify.

User stories and use cases are not everything

Two popular tools for structuring information on tasks that the users will be able to perform in the system are use cases (UCs) and user stories (USs). For now, let me skip the discussion about the differences between UC and US and when to use them[1] and let me move on to a few "did you know thats" about UC and US.

In my work, I have often come across some anti-patterns of forming USs such as these examples:

- As an operator, I want to log in in order to be logged in.
- As a sales rep, I want to generate a monthly report in order to see the monthly statement of sales.
- As an advisor, I want to make a new offer, because the product owner wants it.

Again, for the sake of simplicity, let me skip the discussion of whether each US presented above has actually been uttered by the system user. The thing to observe in these examples is the lack of an unambiguous formulation of the goals of USs. In a moment, you will see that it has some really serious financial implications.

Similar anti-patterns apply to UCs. Experts point to the following weaknesses:

- The UC is too general.
- The UC is too strongly associated with a particular technology.

---

1 Those who are interested should first have a look at Alistair Cockburn's book *Writing Effective Use Cases* and his blog at http://alistair.cockburn.us.

- There are no alternative scenarios.
- The UC is too complex.

Both the UC and US were designed as tools to support collaboration between the business and IT. Their main purpose sometimes disappears from the foreground. Here are a few of my observations about this topic:

- The USs and UCs are treated as an end in themselves. Typically, the final goal of any programming project is to create a product or a service executed by means of software. The ultimate goal[2] is the controlling parameter of listing expectations – in any form. Nevertheless, it is dangerous when the creation of UC or US "detaches" from the software-delivery process and becomes the art for art's sake.

- The UCs and USs are used as a shield against being bothered. In some contexts, the volume of documentation is inversely proportional to the subjectively perceived quality of cooperation of the business and IT. I have witnessed situations in which extensive and detailed UC was created primarily to make developers stop whining.

- There's focus on completing the forms instead of on collaboration. We tend to unreasonably assume that writing down excellent UCs and USs is a guarantee of the project success. We often experience cognitive error called "the social proof".[3] It's amazing that while appreciating the first value of the Agile Manifesto – individuals and interactions over processes and tools[4] – we are also able to give priority to tools. Maybe it's because this time the tools are agile.

- The final business goal of the initiative is not clear enough. As an outcome of this, we have stories or cases that do not align to the business goal. In that situation, the desired features become a bunch of partially or never used[5] software functionalities.

- Even with a written UC or US, it is possible to misunderstand the business needs. There's a joke like that: Three bridges were built in a small town, because only the third time did the bridge builders find the river. You can do a lot of good and costly work without understanding what the project is really about.

USs, UCs, and other methods that shape the desired software features or domain-specific knowledge create a better understanding of what

---

2   There are situations when creating documentation is a vital element of the product business value. We skip them without any harm to this chapter.

3   *Social proof in Influence: The Psychology of Persuasion*, Robert Cialdini.

4   http://www.agilemanifesto.org/

5   http://theagileexecutive.com/2010/01/11/standish-group-chaos-reports-revisited/

the business expects. There are other methods[6] that allow you to model the business reality, possibly in a better way. Here arises the question of where to find the business knowledge, the domain-specific knowledge, and the expectations? The answer is obvious: in the minds of the business people!

If you specifically and concretely know what to do, saving it in any form – USs, UCs, scenarios, models, or any other way – will be easy, and you will even be able to write a script to do it. ☺ The difficult part is to extract the business knowledge from people, to refine expectations, and to separate things that are necessary from those that are only attractive. This is what conversation patterns deal with.

Conversation patterns are methods of managing conversation, asking questions, searching for the needs, and clarifying expectations. These are effective techniques that are used by people who are successful in gaining knowledge from the business. These techniques are named, organized, and described algorithmically to let any IT expert use them right away.

What is a need?

Let's examine something that precedes all conversation patterns. It is the "need". What is a need? Read the following two statements:

- I am responsible for increasing the number of supported contracts to 600 so I want to see a list of monthly contracts.
- If the number of supported contracts remains at the level of 200 per month, the business will shut our department so I want to see a list of monthly contracts.

These statements come from different clients who want the same functionality – to see the list of monthly contracts. The difference between these two statements is the reason why the functionality should be delivered. This reason is called a "business need".

In these examples, the expected functionalities are exactly the same, so what is the difference in the business needs? A closer look will show that the first need is the achievement of a greater number of supported contracts while the second one is preventing the department from being

---

6 http://www.infoq.com/articles/star-driven-approaches

closed. These examples illustrate two groups of business needs: benefits to gain and problems to avoid.

Behind each functionality is either an expected benefit or a problem that needs to be solved. If a business person does not see a chance to gain a benefit or avoiding a problem thanks to implementing a new functionality, it makes no sense to implement it. It makes no sense to pay for it!

If you understand which business needs hide behind the expected functionalities, you will understand what the business appreciates most. This is the business value of the functionality.

It is easy to talk about functionalities, because they are visible. You can draw the user's screen or the control flow. In the case of back-end software, you can draw a diagram of components or specify the API for the module. You can easily name and define these. Finding and naming the needs is a lot more difficult because they are usually hidden.

When you talk with the business people, they initially tell you what they want. They usually do not dictate their needs in simple terms. It is said that the responsibility of business is to determine what is to be done while the responsibility of IT is to determine how to do it. I personally think that this border can be pushed even further. The task of the business is to determine why and for what purpose the software is created while IT may deal with what software and how it works.

Before you start writing stories or use cases...

In my opinion, one of the greatest strengths of software development is that everything is possible. Every piece of functionality might be implemented with some effort. At the same time, this strength is a weakness – the team may deliver even useless features. If you ask for an e-mail client, you will get it; if you ask for a barcode scanner, you will get it; if you want to choose a menu option by clapping your hands – no problem, the team will deliver that, too. There are no limits in software development – everything is possible!

The business goal of the initiative is the critical thing that keeps all desired features aligned to the one goal. This is the reason why the main business goal (product, project) has to be first clarified, understood, and shared by every involved individual.

Let me skip the identification of market expectations and assume that potential customers do indeed desire the new product. The simplest but the most powerful tip for setting an initiative's business goal is quantification.[7] In the example above, I recognized two flavours of need:

- I am responsible for increasing the number of supported contracts to 600….
- If the number of supported contracts remains at the level of 200 per month….

These were already quantified in the dimension of number of contracts, but what about: time boundaries, types of contracts, workers involved, and reality checks? All these aspects will help to quantify the business goal and will bring a better understanding of expected outcomes. You will find the techniques for clarifying business expectations in this and further chapters.

How does the business talk about problems?

Following the division of needs into avoiding problems and gaining benefits, let us assume that you are talking with a business person during a planning meeting. While you are trying to formulate a new US, your interlocutor says, "As a user, I want functionality X, because…":

- "I am afraid that the margin will be calculated incorrectly."
- "That GUI is unintuitive."
- "I don't want the user to have the wrong impression."

You hear a specific emotion in these statements, a negative one: "I'm afraid that…", "I do not want to", etc. Similar examples include:

- "It does not work as it should."
- "It is too slow/hard/etc.…."
- "The problem is that…."

---

7   http://projectmanagement.atwork-network.com/2012/03/20/qa-tom-gilb-on-quantifying-project-objectives/

- "This is impossible, because…."
- "It is difficult, because…."

These phrases obviously indicate that the speaker is trying to describe something he/she wants to avoid. Thus, the speaker describes his/her need in the form of a problem to avoid.

After recognizing the signals that indicate the problem, you have to name the problem. It frequently resembles the following patterns:

- "I want to avoid…"
- "I do not want…"
- "It is difficult because…"
- "If we do not do that, then…"

When you replace the ellipsis with the phrase that describes your problem, the sentence will make sense:

- "I want to avoid incorrectly calculating the margin."
- "I do not want unintuitive GUI."
- "I do not want the user to have the impression that we're cheap."

How does the business talk about benefits?

During a conversation about new functionalities, your interlocutor says, "As a user, I want functionality X, because…":

- "We will be able to design reports on our own."
- "We'll use the salary calculator as soon as possible."
- "We will test this module in a better way."

Just as in the case of problems to solve, in the given statements you hear a characteristic phrase, in this case "we will be able to…," "we will use it as soon as possible," and "we will test something better." Similar phrases include:

- "I expect that…."
- "Thanks to…."
- "It should/must/can/could…."
- "It would be great if…."

Here, you can name the benefit quite easily because in most cases, it fits into one of the following patterns:

- "I want to achieve…."
- "It will make…."
- "This will mean that…."

Calling back to the above examples, we have:

- "It will let us design the reports on our own."
- "This will mean that we'll use the salary calculator as soon as possible."
- "I want to achieve better testing."

User story versus needs

Consider these two common US patterns:

- As <role>, I want <functionality> in order to <goal>.
- In order to <goal>, as <role>, I want <functionality>.

Although similar, each of these two patterns has unique consequences.

Using the first pattern, you start the conversation with a functionality. Because talking about functionalities is easy and natural, you can spend a lot of time on drawing screens, models, or processes. Obviously, these are important actions, but at the end of the day you will want to have the whole US written down. At that point, you will be tempted to use a general formulation in the story rather than the real goal – but it is only the real goal that motivates business to order a particular functionality.

The second pattern will bring a much better effect because you start the conversation by searching for the goal – that is, the business need. When you use the second template, you can start the conversation about functionalities only on condition that you have already clearly defined the needs.

Note that you can use knowledge about the needs to improve the template of the US. Instead of one pattern, you will have two that are more precise:

- In order to avoid <problem to avoid>, as <role>, I want <functionality>.

- In order to achieve <benefit to gain>, as <role>, I want <functionality>.

I use double-sided printed cards for this in practice. One side of the card is for the pattern of gaining benefits, the other for the pattern associated with business problems. With this template, it is easier to recognize the needs behind the requirements signalled by the business. Also, it will be easier for you to manage the conversation and, as a consequence, you will be able to offer a functionality that hits the nail on the head.

Which question did you choose?

Take another look at the first paragraph. Which of the proposed questions did you choose?

What will this chapter be about? This is a question about functionality. If you chose this, you have read the chapter, you have learned its content, and you will soon forget about it.

What was the most difficult part of my recent conversation with the client? This is a valuable question because it highlights the problem that you are struggling with. If you chose this question, you will use this chapter as a source of potential solutions to your problem.

Why do I repeat the same mistakes when talking to the client? This is also a question about a problem, but if you keep asking yourself this question, you will feel worse and worse. Of course, the ability to experience difficult emotions is useful, but in the case of this question there is no reference to the expected result.

What new opportunities would arise if my conversations with clients went the way I want them to go? This is also a valuable question as it relates to potential benefits. If you chose this question, you will use this chapter as a source of inspirations to gain these benefits.

In conclusion, the second and fourth are the recommended questions.

Summary

In this chapter, I presented the foundations for the techniques of discovering needs. You know how to recognize need-like expressions during a conversation but if you've read carefully, you will ask yourself how to know which of the needs expressed by the interlocutor is the real one? This is next step that we will closely examine: asking good questions to clarify the needs.

PART
FIVE

Discovering business needs

When you run a US session and begin to talk about functionalities, you often notice that your interlocutor uses words that are need-like. But which of the needs is the right one?

Questions that probe for needs

Questions are the first tools to use to search for appropriate business needs. Asking a skilful question will allow you to get relevant information. I am absolutely convinced that if a business person does not give you the information you are looking for, it means you yourself have asked the wrong question at the wrong time.

Please, read the previous sentence again. It reveals one of the key assumptions behind this book. I assume that you are fully responsible for carrying out a conversation, you're the professional who will provide the software, and you know what information you need. Without these assumptions, it is easy to burden the business people with the blame for an unsuccessful conversation – and to deem them incapable of communicating effectively. Searching for causes of these problems among the business people does not lead to any meaningful solution – but understanding that it is your own deficiency does!

Since there are two shades of business needs – a problem to avoid and a benefit to gain – there are also two groups of questions that will help you discover these needs.

The basic question that explores the problems your interlocutor is trying to avoid is the "why" question. Trying to answer "why", we usually focus on problems from the past. A similar result is achieved by more specific questions exploring the area of problems to be solved:

- Why is it important?
- What is hard about it?
- What will you prevent?
- What can you lose?
- What are you trying to avoid?
- What might happen if you do not get this functionality?
- How much money can you lose?

Questions of this kind are mostly aimed at clarifying what motivates your interlocutor to want that functionality – in other words, what value the interlocutor attributes to this functionality or, more simply, what business value this functionality has.

The basic question for seeking benefits to gain is "what for?". When you answer it, you usually focus on future benefits, as in specific questions of this kind:

- What will it give you?
- What is the purpose of it?
- What or how much do you have to gain?
- What will happen if we implement it?
- What will be possible then?
- What can you achieve?
- What new opportunities are associated with it?
- What is really new in it?

You may now be wondering where to look for needs. Is it in the direction of problems to avoid or perhaps the direction of benefits to gain? The answer is quite simple: listen to what your interlocutor says. You can start the conversation with some neutral questions:

- What made you want this functionality?
- What is important about this functionality?

Then carefully listen to the answers and look for phrases that indicate the specific type of business need (see the "What is a business need?" chapter). After that, you can start asking questions related to the direction in which the interlocutor has more to say.

Look for specific needs

You may ask, "What made you want this functionality?" and get this response:

"Oh, the feeling that it will be cool!"

Well, maybe it will indeed "be cool" but that doesn't mean it has anything to do with business needs. At this point, a set of precise questions will be helpful:

- How will you know that…?
- How will you measure that…?
- How? In what way?
- What specifically will make you…?
- Who? Where? When? With whom? How much?
- Give an example of….

In the context of precision questioning, it helps to encourage the interlocutor to formulate statements according to the rules of "semantical concretism".[1] Concretism is Tadeusz Kotarbiński's philosophy according to which only those sentences that contain names referring to things existing in reality are valid. Thus, the sentence "It will be cool" is not valid in the sense of semantical concretism but the sentence "Person X will send us the order form" is.

Look for needs associated with a particular business

"Increase in monthly revenue" and "reduction of hidden costs" are more or less valid needs but they apply to almost any business. Look for needs that are specific to the business for which you are creating the software. For example, the user of an online bookstore has the following needs:

- the need not to create a new account (a problem),
- the need not to re-enter all data with every purchase (a problem),
- the need to get the book a day after purchase (a benefit), and
- the need not to pay for the delivery of every single book (a problem).

Some, but not all, of the items from this short list will translate into a functionality as some of them fall outside the realm of the IT system.

Look for needs that motivate

Search for those needs that make your business interlocutor want to stand up and shout, "Yes! That's what I want!" These needs are the ones that

---

1   http://www.ontology.co/kotarbinskit.htm

should be written down in the US. To decide which need is closest to what the business really wants to convey, you may use the following questions:

- What will be the consequences if you avoid it?
- What will be the consequences if you achieve it?
- If you were forced to come to terms with only one problem, which one would you choose?
- If you were able to achieve only one of the benefits, which one would you choose?
- If you were forced to discard a benefit, which one would you choose?

These questions on the one hand help you to detail the consequences of meeting the business needs and on the other hand help you set priorities to determine the most important need.

Discovering the needs in action

Let's combine all the information about discovering needs. Take a conversation between business and developers as an example. Such conversations take place often and, generally speaking, follow the same pattern:

> **Business:** *I'd like to add a button to generate a partial report to this screen.*

> **Developer Team:** *Which data should be displayed? What should it show if there's no data? Is this requirement consistent with the overall vision of the process? Have you thought about the consequences of partial data aggregation? This may require more refactoring.*

> **Business:** *Um, I have to ask....*

Superficially, there is nothing extraordinary about the team's questions – they are just some decent, precise questions. But as usual, the context is the key. In cases such as this one, the team uses a large amount of detailed and sometimes technical questions in order to say no.

When talking with someone from the team, using the questions in the dialogue above is perfectly okay because the team member is sufficiently competent to answer them. When you ask the same questions of people unable to answer them because they do not have adequate knowledge, their responses might even come across as intentionally aggressive. If you want to say no, just say no. This is definitely closer to assertiveness than is torturing your interlocutor with incomprehensible questions. Apart from that, it often happens that the simpler, more direct conversations end with parties convincing each other that a given functionality makes or does not make mutual sense.

Does that mean that you should always avoid this type of question when talking to the business? Of course not! At one point or another, you will have to ask for details. The important thing is to first discover the need – and then ask the more specific or more technical questions.

How could the dialogue presented above proceed more effectively? Follow the progression of this new conversation from top to bottom by row.

Business	Team	Comment
"I'd like to add a button to generate a partial report to this screen."	(No comment.)	Stop. Even if you are absolutely convinced that this requirement is unreasonable or makes no sense at all, stop. Do not argue, do not convince. Discover the need.
	"What do you expect to gain with this partial report?"	
"I don't want to wait until the end of the month for the sales charts."		The team inquired about a potential benefit, but the business pointed out a problem to avoid. Yes, it can happen, and in such cases you need to follow your interlocutor's lead.
	"So the key is the time you have to wait for sales charts?"	
"Yes!"		

Table 5.1. Effective communication between team and business.

At this point, a business need has been identified as a problem to avoid: "I don't want to wait until the end of the month for the sales charts."

Having identified the need, you can proceed to define its acceptance criteria. In other words, you have to determine how your interlocutor will know that the problem has been solved or that the benefit has been achieved. Why is it so important to formulate acceptance criteria? I'll hit that in a moment.

Team: *To stay up to date, which particular charts would you like to see and how often?*

Business: *I'd need charts of key clients twice a week.*

If the team wanted to sum up what they have just learned from the client, it would be something like "I want to avoid waiting until the end of the month for the sales charts, and I will avoid that if I'm able to see the sales charts of key clients twice a week."

With this knowledge, the team can continue the conversation.

Team: *Oh! So we can do this or this or that. Which of these solutions is in your opinion the best??*

Business: *That second one looks interesting!*

The team tried to identify the need and determine its acceptance criteria in order to be able to suggest alternative solutions. That is the magic behind the needs.

The most common tactics for dealing with new functionalities that do not fit into the architecture are providing arguments in order to persuade and force your own ideas. When you focus on needs in the first place, it allows you to find an alternative solution that will both satisfy the business and be acceptable to the team.

PART
SIX

Conversation structure

Have you ever seen a file with application-server diagnostic information (in short, logs)? Figure 6.1 presents such a file.

Figure 6.1. (Il)legible application-server log.

For many people, such a log is simply a large amount of text that means nothing. However, people who often work with this kind of file will find lots of useful information there. They know how to look at seemingly incomprehensible data to pick out what is most important for them (e.g. entries of [ERROR] or [FATAL] and specific queries to the database). The same applies to conversations about new features, changes in existing functionalities, or changes in the rules of operation of the business for which we develop software. In the course of such conversations, people talk a lot – and "smuggle in" pieces of information. The people are more or less accurate. To pick out what is essential to deliver the software, you need to be able to listen and disect the conversation in an appropriate manner.

Conversation has a structure

Since source code can be structured (in the form of design patterns) in a way that makes it easier to develop and maintain, why not apply the same practice to a conversation? When I consider a conversation in a structured and orderly manner, it may help me lead it more effectively. What I mean here is not related to patterns of conducting meetings, during which every participant has their specific role. I am talking about something more fundamental – about how people exchange information (especially people from the business to those in IT) in the course of a conversation. I assume that your interlocutor does not need to have any knowledge about the techniques of gathering information or conducting meetings. I only assume that he/she has the will to say what he/she knows.

Let's assume that you're developing software for the healthcare industry, and you're interviewing one of the key users (a physician) on the functionality of writing prescriptions in the new software. The conversation goes as follows:

> **You:** *How are you going to use this tool?*
>
> **User:** *Well, the most important thing for me is to enter the appropriate dosage of the medication as quickly as I could do it with a paper prescription. Have you ever seen a paper prescription?*
>
> **You:** *Of course.*
>
> **User:** *You know, paper prescriptions are very flexible. I can write whatever I want. This new functionality should be equally flexible. By the way, our employees have a few problems with the new system.*
>
> **You:** *Okay, so you want to write a prescription using ordinary text. What else?*
>
> **User:** *The prescription must be linked to the drug cabinet. The cabinet is a fairly complex issue. The key is to meet the requirements of the Legal Act XYZ. In the case of prescriptions, we are also obliged to comply with several regulations.*

Imagine that the conversation is similar in its structure to the one in Figure 6.2.

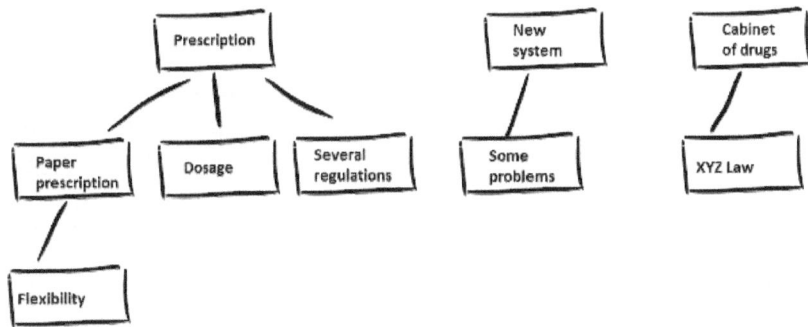

Figure 6.2. The structure of the conversation.

All the pieces of information that you can get are governed by a need, i.e. the reason why a person from the business requires this functionality. Next, imagine that you can organize those crucial pieces of information on a tree structure: there is general information at the top and concrete information at the bottom.

Let's take the conversation's tree structure and mark the order in which different pieces of information appear.

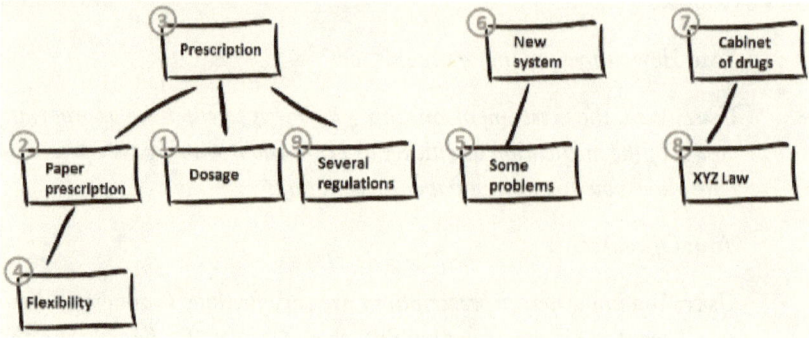

Figure 6.3. Information order of appearance.

The first information relates to "dosage" and the next to "paper prescription". Both were given in the context of the "prescription". Next, the user spoke of the "flexibility" of a paper prescription and about "some problems" with the "new system". Then, the user mentioned a "drug cabinet" and "Legal Act XYZ" that regulates its use. At the end, the user also mentioned that the prescriptions are bound by "several regulations".

The course of the conversation

The thing you'll notice once you visualize the conversation is its course (see figure 6.4). This conversation was chaotic! I use the word "chaotic" not to judge it but to label the specific properties of this particular conversation and to distinguish it from a structured conversation. In this sample conversation, the interlocutors spontaneously moved from concrete to general remarks and changed the topic. This is how people speak to each other and that's somewhat natural.

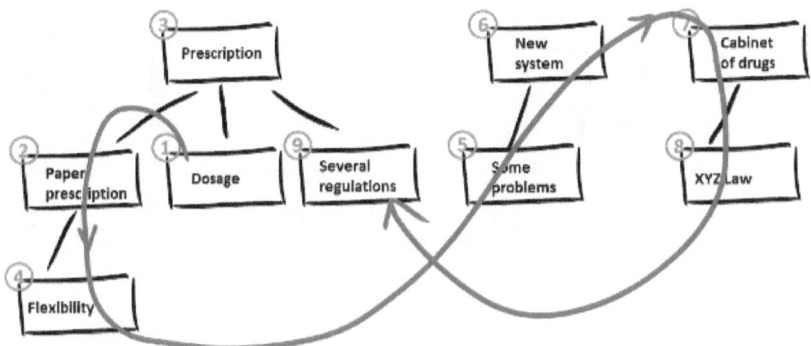

Figure 6.4. The course of the conversation.

This quasi-natural way of speaking with people is not always effective if your goal is to determine what the business is ready to pay for. If you run a conversation in a chaotic manner, it may be that:

- You collect a lot of information but little knowledge.
- You only slightly understand what is happening in the business.
- You have chaotic notes.
- You think that you should do something, but you are not sure what exactly needs to be done.

Steering the course of the conversation

We can distinguish three basic ways to navigate the conversation structure (see figure 6.5):

- up (summarizing), which aims to find the need hidden behind the interlocutor's expectations;
- down (concretizing), which aims to formulate acceptance criteria for the expectations of the interlocutor; and
- to the side (building analogy), which aims to identify a particularly difficult subject in a different context and to move the conclusions back to the original context.

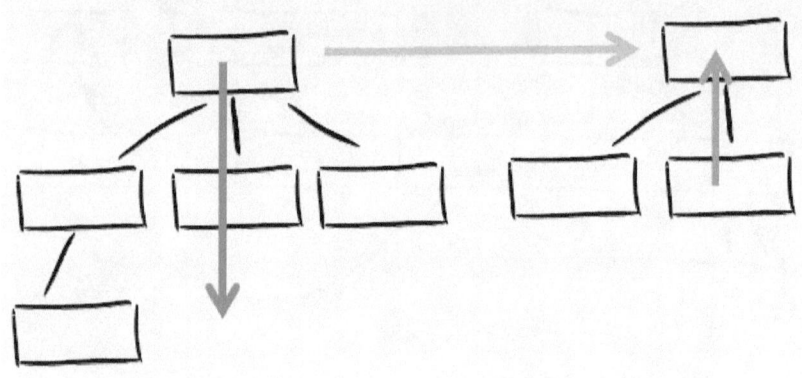

Figure 6.5. Directions of navigation through the conversation structure.

Notice that discovering business needs is in fact steering the conversation up – from specific solutions to needs. You can read about methods for that purpose in the previous chapters. I will now focus on concretizing, i.e. going down in the structure of the conversation.

Concretizing is about getting concrete information. In software development, concrete information relates to acceptance criteria, acceptance testing, functional testing, UCs, USs, interface sketches, and examples of output data.

The boundary between general information and concrete information is quite conventional. It frequently happens that we perceive concrete things as those that can be measured, i.e. something that can be reduced to a number. From this perspective, the criterion of "an intuitive user interface" is not concrete, while the information that "the screen contains no more than five control units" is. Another criterion of concreteness is the number of designates. Most of the concepts that appear in the course of the conversation have their designates, i.e. objects existing in reality, which are referred to by a specific name. The fewer designates there are, the greater the concreteness of a given concept. Thus, a phrase like "the main problem is the weak test" is not concrete, while a phrase like "our main concern is that we achieve a 100% code coverage when testing getters and setters" is much more concrete.

Of course, you can concretize any information down to the level of a pixel or even an atom, but at some point it will become an art for art's sake. For this reason, the importance of concretizing lies in the context of the conversation – the context that is assumed a priori by those who take part in it. To some people, the idea of "the standard login screen" is quite clear because they have specific contextual knowledge that allows them to correctly understand that formulation.

One of your most important tasks is to verify whether the context that you assume for the duration of the conversation is in line with the reality – or not. For example, an obvious and rarely challenged assumption is that the person I talk to knows what the conversation will be about and is prepared for it. That often turns out to be a false assumption. A good idea is to start accepting as few assumptions as possible, and then to gradually increase them in order to facilitate the conversation.

Having outlined the difference between the general and the concrete, it is time to think about the details. We tend to perceive the collection of requirements as collecting detailed information. Detailed information is not the same as concrete information. "Concrete" means "well-defined, accurate, precise" and "detailed" means "containing many details". Concrete information will often be detailed, but detailed information does not have to be concrete.

An example of this is the documentation generated by reverse-engineering tools based on the source code. The large amount of documentation generated this way contains many details – so it is detailed. At the same time, it is rarely concrete. The aim of interviews with people from the business is to gather concrete information, not detailed information. Of course, you will get a lot of details – most often as a side effect of the search for concrete information – but you should focus primarily on the concrete ones. Remember that.

How to ask for concrete information

As in the case of searching for needs, the key here is to ask the right questions in the right way. Questions that concretize concepts and lead your interlocutor down the structure of the conversation are:

- How? How exactly? What exactly?
- What does it consist of?
- How do you measure it?
- How much? When? Where? With whom?

- How do you know that?
- Give an example of….
- In what order?

By asking these questions, you encourage your interlocutor to break down the general information into more concrete information. By doing this, you go down the structure of the conversation in two ways (see figure 6.6): into its breadth and into its depth.

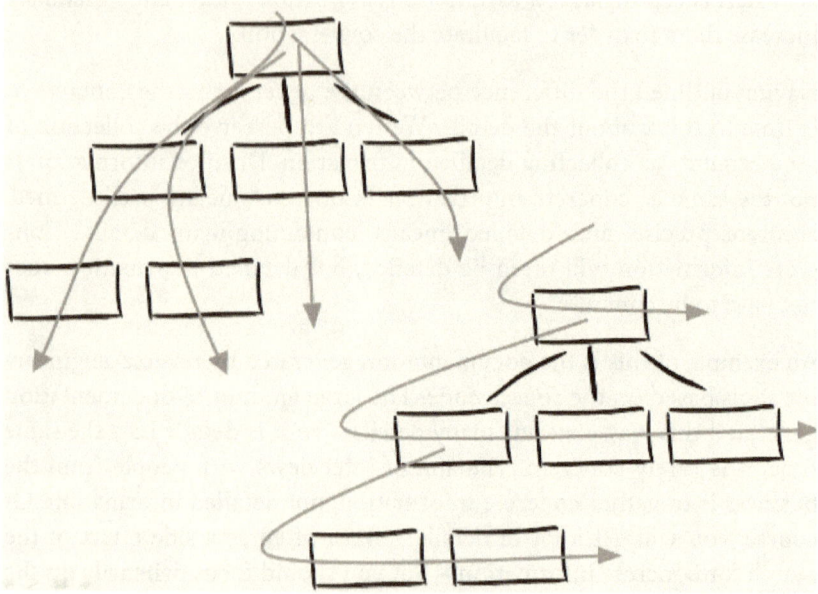

Figure 6.6. Going down the conversation structure by depth (blue arrows) and breadth (green arrows).

Going into the depth is a focus on a single topic and thoroughly exploring it. The most common effect of this approach is that you will learn a lot about one topic and little or nothing about other potentially important issues. People conducting conversation this way often say that they "floated" into a given topic.

Going into the breadth of the structure of the conversation usually gives better results, because this familiarizes you with the entire issue and not only a small part of it. Due to time constraints, you will have to intertwine concretizing questions with questions about priorities like "Which of the topics are we going to cover now?"

Let's see in table 6.1 how to conduct a sample conversation with a user about new software if you use concretizing questions and navigate the breadth of the conversation's structure.

You	User (Physican)	Comment
"How would you like to create a prescription in the system?"		Originally, this question was "How are you going to use this tool?" By the words "use" and "tool", you focus the attention of your interlocutor on a fairly wide range of function-alities. To limit the scope, make this question more concrete, one that clearly indicates that you're only asking about a "prescrip-tion in the system".
-	"The most important thing is to enter the appro-priate dosage as quickly as I could with a paper pre-scription. Have you ever seen a paper prescription?"	The user ended his utterance with a question. Questions have the power to prompt the interlocutor to immediately answer them or to think about the answer. In the course of a conversation about requirements, it is distract-ing. Do not go for it.
"We'll talk about paper prescriptions in a moment. But for now, is the idea of writing the appropri-ate dosage quickly all that you expect from the functionality of delivering prescriptions with the system?	-	The first sentence sus-pends the topic of paper prescriptions in order to examine whether there are any other expectations. This way, you go down into the breadth of the conversation structure to check whether the interlocutor wants to add something.

You	User (Physican)	Comment
-	"I have to check what drugs the patient is already taking, because certain drugs cannot be combined with each other. I would like the system to detect such interactions. Another important thing is flexibility. Then, there's that drug cabinet…."	A new expectation arises: detecting interactions between drugs. At this point, there is some ambiguity in the vocabulary used. Can you talk about "creating" prescriptions, or about "writing" them? Be sure to clarify what these two actions mean and how they differ. For the sake of simplicity, let's omit this ambiguity.
"How will you know that creating prescriptions in the system is flexible enough?"	-	Now you concretize the general information about the prescription's "flexibility".
-	"Well, that I'll be able to write them by hand."	The user perceives "flexibility" as doing exactly the same thing as before, and the system will somehow help.
"In sum, you want to enter the name and dosage of medication by hand, just like on a paper prescription. The system should inform you about potential interactions between drugs. The dosage should be appropriate and, if I understand correctly, delivering prescriptions should be in some way linked to the drugs cabinet. Is that all?"	-	-
-	"In principle, yes."	-
"Okay. So, I would like to clarify….	-	-

Table 6.1. A conversation with a physician.

To practice your skills, try to map the structure and course of the above conversation following the diagrams in this chapter.

You may now be wondering how to ask a question that motivates the interlocutor to give exactly the information that you want, how to skilfully interrupt your interlocutor if he/she strays from the topic, or how to make sure that you properly understand a given business concept. The next chapter will focus on different types of questions that hit the nail on the head.

PART
SEVEN

Questions that hit the nail on the head

You already know the techniques that help to define and clarify the actual business needs that hide behind the expected functionalities and USs. The current chapter is about asking questions that hit the nail on the head.

Look at the following three fragments of conversations between the product owner and the team.

Conversation 1:

> **Team:** *Are we changing anything in the next sprint?*
>
> **Product owner:** *I don't think so....*

Conversation 2:

> **Team:** *What would you like to change in the next sprint?*
>
> **Product owner:** *Hmmm... I haven't thought about it yet.*

Conversation 3:

> **Team:** *Which stories from the backlog are still linked to the objective of the next sprint?*
>
> **Product owner:** *Have we talked about the objective?*

Each of these conversations is the same thing: the team wants to know what to work on in the near future. However, the conversation will probably proceed in various directions, depending on the question and response:

- In conversation 1, the dialogue will immediately end and no sprint-scope analysis will take place; perhaps the topic will re-emerge after breaking down the USs into tasks or during work or a demonstration of the product.
- Conversation 2 will highly likely lead to additional backlog grooming; it is possible that USs or scenarios will be added to the scope of the next sprint.
- After conversation 3, it is possible that the whole team will be informed of the objective and will participate in backlog grooming that features the objective.

The immediate cause of each direction of the conversations is the question the team asked. In stories about cooperation during a project's lifetime, you often find statements like "the product owner did not say that", "the team did not inform us", "vaguely described requirements", "they do not know what they want", and the like. In general, interlocutors claim that they have received inadequate information on planned tasks. This universal habit of making your interlocutors responsible for inaccurate conversations has turned into your metric: the quality of the information obtained indicates the quality of the questions asked.

Isn't it a great tool for improving cooperation? From now on, instead of saying "the product owner did not say that", you should say "I did not ask the product owner about that"; instead of saying "the team did not inform us", you should say with conviction "we *never asked the tam about it*"; instead of saying "vaguely described requirements", say simply "I did not ask enough questions"; and instead of complaining that "they do not know what they want", consent to the fact that you cannot simply get information about needs and requirements. Only once you have been armed with effective questions can you work on improving them and thus improve cooperation during the project.

Hitting the nail on the head

When we look at communication, we come to a conviction that every person has a module that can be called the "buffer of useless answers". A buffer is a place from which your interlocutor derives answers when you ask imprecise or messy questions. A buffer is a buffer – it can include anything:

- last used responses like "Okay, okay;"
- fragments of conversations like "Good, let's use a NoSQL database;"
- unrelated memories like "Do it like we did in the old system;" or
- standard conversation endings like "I will consider it and we'll talk about it next time" or "Ask John."

If you want useful information from the interlocutor, your most important task is to ask questions that bypass the buffer of useless answers.

Choose the directions
in a conscious way

Suppose you want to learn a little more about the operation of a travel agency. What kind of questions will you ask? How does a travel agent work? How does a travel agency operate? What happens at a travel agency? Or maybe you'll ask some other questions. Each of these questions will be followed by a slightly different answer. Let's see why.

- *How does a travel agent work?* It is likely that the interlocutor will hear the word "agent" and refer to his/her own work in a travel agency. He/she will probably talk about the daily activities that will come to mind during the conversation.

- *How does a travel agency operate?* This question forces the interlocutor to look at the travel agency as a whole. As a result, the answer will talk about the principles underlying the operation of the office, cooperation with external suppliers, etc.

- *What happens at a travel agency?* This question highlights everyday interactions, therefore you will learn a lot about individual tasks and problems, and probably little about individual employees.

Which of the questions is the most appropriate? It depends on what you want to find out. Say you are interested in the business process behind a travel agency:

- Do not ask, "What does it look like?" because the looks are not important to you.

- Do not ask, "How does it work?" because that does not lead the interlocutor to focus on the process.

- Do not ask, "What happens…?" because this question gives the interlocutor the opportunity to talk about anything.

- Do not ask about the "business process" because this is a term coined by analysts that might sound smart but does not mean anything to most people.

- Do ask, "What activities are conducted at a travel agency one after the other?" because this question prompts a description of the nature of the process.

- Do ask, "What happens from the moment a customer enters the office to the moment he/she receives a plane ticket?" because this question refers to a specific process with a clearly marked beginning and end.

Many ambiguities in requirements gathered in a conversation result from improper questions asked during the conversation. The questions are too general, they do not relate to the merits, or they inadvertently induce the speaker to talk about something different than the important topics.

"Is" or "should be"?

In the course of client interviews, I have noticed that when I ask about the business process in which they take part, almost everyone tells how it should function instead of telling how it actually functions at the moment. For this reason, I ask from time to time "Is it actually working the way you describe it? How does it function in your daily practice?" After that, the client usually begins to talk about problems.

Recognize the distinction between how it is and how it should be. Since you build software to support business processes, these processes should be real. It may turn out that the business processes are not optimal and must be modified, but you can notice that only when you find out how they really work.

Must/should/could/may be done

Pay attention to the conditional words "may", "could", "should", "must", and others used by the client. Each of these words reflects a different shade of priority. "Must" has the highest priority, then there is "should", then "could", and finally "may". But here comes a little nuance. For politeness reasons (at least in Polish), you often use "should" in the sense and instead of "must". This is why you have to make sure how critical the requirements are and which of them must/should/etc. be done. You can do it by asking questions such as "So it must be done? Meaning the system makes no sense without this functionality?"

Past, future, and present tense

By asking questions relating to a particular moment in time, you can control both the attention and the activity of your interlocutor:

In the past tense, the interlocutor recalls his daily activities. The past tense is a good way to learn what's really going on. By asking questions such as "How did it work?", "Did this approach bring results?", and "What were your impressions after using it?", you focus the attention of your interlocutors on past experiences in which they actually took part. This allows you to learn the true current state of affairs instead of learning how things should be.

In the present tense, the interlocutor imagines that he/she is taking part in an event. You should use the present tense to discuss UCs, scenarios, and user screens. Ask questions like "What does this screen look like?" and "What appears when you click the Okay button?" Use the present tense even when it is not completely natural or grammatically correct, e.g. "When you click the Options menu, what window do you see?" By asking what window shows up now, you force your interlocutors to adopt a user's perspective – they imagine themselves performing actions and seeing results. This perspective allows them to precisely define their own expectations. The situation changes if the second part of your question is "what window will you see?" with the future tense. Referring to the future turns an interlocutor into an observer of several alternative scenarios rather than a user of just one. In such a context, the interlocutor would probably focus on how something could look rather than does look and therefore would consider several options.

The future tense focuses on benefits and goals. Ask questions like "What will you gain?" and "What will you achieve?"

Use past tense	Use present tense	Use future tense
• When you want to identify the problems of your interlocutor.	• When you define UCs and scenarios.	• When you want to identify the business goals of the client.
• When you want to gather information on the actual situation of the interlocutor.	• When you design user screens with the interlocutor.	• When you want to identify the benefits to be ensured by the software.
	• When you want to learn how the application should function.	

Table 7.1. What tense to use to form questions.

You can combine tenses in one utterance to direct the attention of your interlocutor and to allow yourself to thoroughly understand the requirements, e.g.: *"Up to this point, you've chosen employees from a multi-level menu*

– and it has been a nuisance. Now, you can click on the icon and immediately see the form for adding an employee. Will this really improve your work?"

Ask, don't suggest

Table 7.2 presents a conversation about the requirements of a system supporting the operation of a travel agency. This conversation illustrates several mistakes that I've described.

Developer	Client	Comment
-	"I would like a system to support the operation of a travel agency."	
"Is it supposed to be a system serving one agency or several agencies that cooperate with each other?"	-	The developer suggested a solution, which he initially thought of. This question should be asked much later, after the analyst already understands the customer's business. Raising this issue at this point broadens the scope of the system and lengthens the analytical work but does not guarantee that customer will accept the price and the solution.

It would be more appropriate at this stage to ask if the client runs one or more travel agencies. This question does not suggest any answers but does clue in the developer to the later stages of collecting requirements. |
| - | "Well, all in all, I plan to grow, so it would be good if the system handled several agencies." | The client has become interested in the suggested solution. |

Developer	Client	Comment
"What does the work of a travel agency look like? What is important?"	-	This question is not very specific. It is better to ask what customer service activities the agency performs in sequence.
-	"The customer can drop by the office or buy a trip online. All trips we sell must come from the systems of large tour operators because we are only a mediator in this process. We do not organize trips on our own."	The client signalled two processes of running the service: in the office and online. The developer should explore these processes as soon as possible.
"So we're talking about modules: the module of a normal web service and the module of integration with large tour operators, right?"	-	The developer has transformed the processes into "modules". This loses their dynamic nature and it will be more difficult to determine the sequence of actions performed by the travel agency.
-	"Yes, but I would also like to be able to quickly find deals of the different travel agencies. They could be displayed as a list or a tree structure."	The client makes a big jump to details. At this point, the appearance of the screen (as list or tree) is not the most important thing to address. However, the client has signalled an important quality criterion: the ability to quickly and easily find deals from all large travel agencies.

Table 7.2. Suggestions distort the process of collecting information.

If you want to know the real needs of your interlocutor, you have to focus on asking questions without suggesting the answers.

Close-ended and open-ended questions

Let's start with two definitions.

Close-ended questions are those that have only preconceived answers:

- "Would you like to talk about the new module now?" has two possible answers: yes or no.
- "Do you prefer to have this meeting now or tomorrow at four o'clock?" has two possible answers: now or tomorrow at four.
- "Do you think .NET, JEE, or PHP is more suitable for this project?" has three possible answers: .NET, Java, or PHP.

Open-ended questions are those that have less-constrained answers:

- "How in your opinion should we approach the technological side of this project?"
- "What do you think about your work with this system?"
- "How would you improve your software development process?"

If the distinguishing feature between close-ended and open-ended questions is the possibility of replying with an unconstrained answer (or not), these two types of questions stand at two extreme poles.

Somewhere in between, there are questions that we could call "narrowed questions" – i.e. questions that allow a more or less unconstrained answer but which also impose a strictly defined, narrow scope of response:

- "What problems does the authorization module have?"
- "What should be improved in the process of customer service?"
- "What has to happen in order to serve the customer, starting from the moment he enters the bank and finishing with the moment he leaves with the bank-transfer receipt in his hand?"

Note that the main distinction between these three types of questions is the space that you leave for your interlocutor to fit the answers. The close-ended questions have the smallest space; the open-ended questions have the largest.

Close-ended, narrowed, and open-ended questions are additional tools that you can use to lead the session of collecting requirements and to move around the structure of the conversation in a way that you deem most appropriate. Table 7.3 offers some tips on how to use these questions.

Type	Use when	Example
Close-ended	You want to summarize and eventually concretize expectations. You want to choose between several alternatives. You are defining the conditions for the acceptance of a solution.	"I understand that on this screen the user must have the possibility of doing X, Y, Z. Am I right?" "Should we use JEE or PHP?" "If X, Y, and Z are performed, will you consider the task done?"
Narrowed	You want to go down (to the smaller pieces of information) in the structure of the conversation. You want the customer's answer to have a clearly defined structure.	"What are the most important things in module X?" "What has to happen in order to serve the customer, starting from the moment he enters the bank and finishing with the moment he leaves with a bank-transfer receipt in his hand?"
Open-ended	You start the conversation You want to extract large pieces of information. You want to hear the customer's feedback on a particular topic. You want your customer to speak out. You want to make the atmosphere less tense.	"How can I help?" "What do you expect from this project?" "What prompted you to change the system?" "Has anything interesting happened since the last meeting?"

Table 7.3. When to use close-ended, narrowed, and open-ended questions.

PART EIGHT

How to convince your client to back your ideas

How to convince your client/supervisor/team of your ideas is one of the most common questions that comes up during my work with teams. In this chapter, you will learn effective techniques for proposals that you think are better than those suggested by your client. We will also decide if it is really about convincing.

Take a look at an excerpt from a conversation in table 8.1.

Client	Software professional
"Can you add another button to generate a partial report on this screen?"	-
-	"What data should it show? What should it show if there are no data to display? Have you thought about the consequences of aggregating partial data? This may require serious refactoring!"
"Okay.... Maybe I will think this over first."	-

Table 8.1. A conversation about a certain button.

The client asked a question that virtually every software professional has heard: "Can you do more?" This chapter is more concerned with the reaction of the software professional, who here asks a large number of questions to specify the business expectations. That appears to be a rational reaction. Nonetheless, if you take a closer look at the reaction of the client, who withdraws from the conversation, you may start to have doubts.

A non-technical person such as a client perceives the asking of a lot of detailed questions (I know cases where the number of questions in a single e-mail dangerously approached a hundred) as aggressive behaviour. Think about your last visit to a car mechanic, an electrician, or – more dramatically – a doctor. How did you feel when the specialist communicated the diagnosis to you using a large number of incomprehensible words that sound like "blah blah-blah-blah-blah three thousand?"

Pause for a moment to contemplate this uneasy feeling of helplessness and dependence. Do you see what I mean that asking the client about a number of technical issues is perceived as aggressive? The members of your technical team are another matter. You can ask thousands of technical questions of them and it will still result in a quality conversation. They are prepared to answer such questions and have the necessary knowledge. The client, however, does not have this knowledge.

I sometimes notice that team ask many questions as a tactic to passively say no or to move deadlines. The first technique of this chapter is to be direct: if you want to say "no" then say "no". If you want to say "later", say "later". Saying "no" is being assertive. This may not please the client and might trigger a fierce discussion or tough negotiations. The advantage of a direct "no" is that all parties know where everybody stands and can start looking for solutions. Saying "no" indirectly, by asking a lot of questions is aggressive and directs a client's attention to entirely irrelevant details. That certainly does not add business value.

Since I urge you to avoid asking a lot of technical questions, you might wonder how you should propose an alternative (and, in your opinion, better) solution to your client? It all boils down to the purpose of such questions. If you want to clarify something, you ask different questions than when you want to move the deadline. Secondly, and this is the focus of this chapter, you can suggest alternatives and ask technical questions, but at the right time.

Discover the need

In previous chapters, I wrote in detail about what needs are, how to recognize them, and how to extract them.

Table 8.2 summarizes the most important information about needs.

The need is:	Problem to be solved	Benefit desired	Auxiliary questions
Specific	"I want to avoid…."	"I want to achieve…."	"How will you know that?" "What exactly?" "How? In what way? What will make you…?" "Who? Where? When? With whom? How much? How far?" "Give an example."
Connected with business	"Why?" "Why is it important?" "What would happen if you don't get it?" "What makes you want this?" "What is difficult about it?" "What can you lose?" "What do you want to protect yourself from?" "What are you trying to avoid?"	"What for?" "What will it give to you?" "What can you gain?" "What is the purpose of it?" "What happens when you get it?" "What becomes possible then?" "What new or different thing will it bring?" "What advantage can you thus achieve?"	"How is this related to your work/business?" "How is it related to your business objectives?"
Motivating	The client says: "I do not want to…." "It works too slowly." "It's not intuitive." "The problem is…." "It's difficult, because…." "I am afraid that…."	The client says: "I really care about…." "As a result, I will be able to…." "It will become possible to…." "This will mean that…." "The profit in it is…." "I'm glad, because it will…." "It will be…."	"What are the consequences of avoiding it?" "What are the consequences of achieving it?" "If you were forced to come to terms with only one problem, which would you choose?" "If you were able to achieve only one of the benefits, which would you choose?" "If you were forced to discard one of the benefits, which would you choose?"

Table 8.2. Discovering business needs in a nutshell.

First, discover and name the client's need, then go on to suggesting alternatives – this is the main principle of talking with clients. Figure 8.1 illustrates this pattern of action.

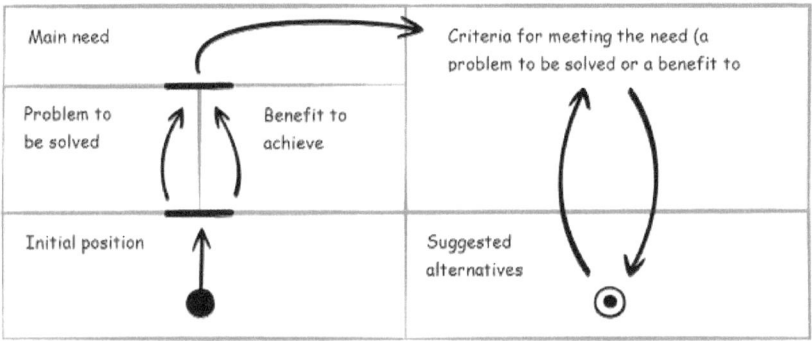

Figure 8.1. Suggesting alternative solutions.

The first step is to determine the position of the client – that is, answering the question "What does the client declare as wanted?" The second step is to discover the client needs that hide behind that position. According to table 8.2, these may be benefits to achieve or problems to be solved. Next, name the main need, which should be classified as specific, connected to the business, or motivating.

My observations indicate that we tend to propose alternative solutions immediately after identifying the position of the client. This most often leads to conflict – Not in the sense of an argument but by forming polarized positions and throwing arguments at each other.

The third step is a bit difficult. It is a moment at which you need to define the criteria for meeting the need, i.e. the criteria That indicates that you have solved the problem or achieved the benefit. Criteria are nothing but acceptance tests for the need. They show how the client will know that the need has been met. Only after naming the needs and defining acceptance criteria does the right moment to propose an alternative and more appropriate solution to the client come.

Sometimes, even after naming needs and defining acceptance criteria, the client does not agree to the solution you have suggested. This only means that there are still some criteria that you have not recognized. To discover those, simply ask "What else, apart from <known criteria>, has to happen to achieve/avoid <need>?"

Table 8.3 illustrates the conversation about the extra button, first presented above, which has been managed according to the pattern of alternative solutions shown in table 8.2.

Client	Software professional	Comments
"Can you add another button to generate a partial report on this screen?"	-	The client declares his/her initial position. The software professional would like to offer a solution that is, in his/her opinion, better, but...
-	"Why do you need this? What would you like to achieve with this report?"	...he/she first focuses on discovering the need that encouraged the client to request this functionality. The software professional asks about the expected benefits, and the client...
"I don't want to wait until the end of the month for the sales charts."	-	...responds with a problem that he/she is trying to avoid. It happens. Generally, people will not respond to the questions. Rather, they will talk about what they know. If you ask a question about the benefit and the client talks about problems, follow the client.
-	"So the problem here is waiting a long time for the sales charts?"	The software professional names the need: "waiting a long time for the sales charts".
"Yes!"	-	-
-	"Which sales charts do you need the most?"	The software professional wants to formulate acceptance criteria for the need discovered – i.e. he/she wants to know how the client will recognize that the problem has been solved.
"I want the sales to key clients."	-	-
-	"If you get an e-mail with these charts, would that be okay? Could we forget about this extra button then?"	Having the criterion in the form of "sales to key clients", the software professional suggests an alternative solution but...

Client	Software professional	Comments
"Well, no. Because with a button, I could have the charts whenever I want while the e-mail makes me dependent on you."	-	… the client does not accept it. This means that there are still some undefined acceptance criteria that…
-	"Tell me how often you need to view the charts with sales to key clients if once per month is too infrequent."	…have to be clarified.
"At least once every two weeks."	-	Another criterion is the frequency of viewing reports.
-	"So, would getting an automated e-mail with these charts every two weeks be enough for you?"	Once again, the software professional considers all acceptance criteria that have been defined so far and proposes an alternative solution.
"I think so. At least for now."	-	Bingo! Just in case, the client adds that this is a solution "for now". Well, the business is changing. ;)

Table 8.3. A conversation about a certain button.

So, what do you think – is this chapter about convincing? Technically speaking, the software professional has changed the client's mind, so he/she has "convinced" him. Note, however, that this has been associated with the identification and understanding of the client's needs – and not with providing the right number of arguments. Arguments are helpful in confirming beliefs of people who are already convinced of their decisions. In contrast, discovering needs and defining acceptance criteria are necessary to find a solution beneficial to both the client and you.

PART
NINE

Is there a kind of chemistry between us?

All the techniques for conducting conversations with clients presented in previous chapters can be called the mechanics of conversation. Using them will have a clear effect. But if there is no chemistry between the interlocutors during the conversation, these mechanics will not operate. The interlocutor will simply have no desire to cooperate.

Nonviolent communication (NVC) is an approach developed by Marshall Rosenberg to assist in caring for this chemistry during conversations. From a technical point of view, NVC is a method of conducting dialogues. However, apart from specific techniques, it advocates a set of assumptions and beliefs that might motivate you to think of NVC as a philosophy of treating another human being – and a philosophy for which verbal communication is the medium.

Learn to observe

"You're pissing me off!"

What is your first reaction to the above message? Surprise? Anger? Annoyance? NVC specifies more precise and flexible tools to maintain contact with anyone who spits out such a message.

Think first about what made the other person shout "You're pissing me off!" If you come up with answers like you did something that angered or irritated him or you were late... – stop. You are speaking in generalizations and you've taken the words of your interlocutor to heart.

Imagine that you are looking at a conversation with the interlocutor from the point of view of an observer, like a scientist observing a swarm of ants in a terrarium. Behold the path that lead your interlocutor to accuse you of pissing him/her off.

The NVC communication model states that at the beginning, there is an observation. An observation is a sentence that starts with:

- "I saw...",
- "I heard...",
- "I said...", or
- "I did..." (physically).

What could your interlocutor see/hear/say/do that made him/her scream, "You're pissing me off!"? He/she could have, for example, seen that you entered the meeting room five minutes after the beginning of the meeting or heard you say that his/her idea made no sense.

From the point of view of NVC, however, the interlocutor was certainly not able to see that you were late for a meeting or hear you criticize his/her ideas.

"Be late" and "criticize" are not observations but evaluations. "Coming five minutes after the appointed time" is often called "being late" and "saying that the idea makes no sense" is sometimes called "criticism". But these shorthand labels in no way describe what has actually (and in most cases physically) happened. Therefore, the NVC model goes for observations rather than evaluations.

Recognize the human need

"You're pissing me off!"

You already know that before the interlocutor shouted these words, he/she saw that you came to the meeting five minutes after the appointed time or heard that you called his/her idea pointless.

Let's continue the investigation. What happened immediately after the interlocutor observed these situations?

Here we come to the crux of NVC: the needs. Needs, as perceived in NVC, are universal – i.e. common to all people. Look at the needs listed in table 9.1. Nearly every person in the world seeks these needs. Marshall Rosenberg writes that the needs are what are alive in us. Because of the universality of these needs and the necessity to distinguish them from the business needs that I referred to earlier, I will call these "human needs".

- Freedom of choice of dreams, goals, and values
- Freedom of choice of plans
- Celebrating development
- Mourning losses
- Authenticity
- Creativity
- Meaning
- Feeling of personal worth
- Acceptance
- Recognition
- Closeness
- Community
- Significance
- Empathy
- Honesty
- Love
- Joy
- Support
- Respect
- Trust
- Understanding
- Having fun
- Laughter
- Beauty
- Harmony
- Inspiration
- Order
- Peace
- Rest
- Shelter
- Food

Table 9.1. Human needs as perceived in Rosenberg's NVC.

NVC holds that ineffective communication, conflict, negative feelings, and behaviours arise as a direct result of unmet human needs. The essence of NVC is the ability to recognize, name, and talk about the needs of yours and others because then, instead of pointing out each other's mistakes, we are in a conversation about what we value most – our human needs.

Saying phrases like these is explicitly talking about human needs:

- I need peace of mind.
- I am tired.
- I need support in the near future.
- I need to understand the meaning of this project.

On the other hand, look at these phrases:

- I need you to leave.
- I need to finish this project.
- I need to change jobs.
- Leave me alone!
- This project does not make sense!

With these, you are not talking about needs. The statements refer to specific solutions – "to leave", "to finish this project", "to change jobs" – that are intended to meet distinct needs. Nevertheless, those actual needs remain unnamed.

Learn to name feelings

"You're pissing me off!"

You now know that before the interlocutor shouted these words, he/she saw that you came to the meeting five minutes after the appointed time or heard that you called his/her idea pointless.

NVC tells you that this really means that one of human needs important to the interlocutor – let's assume that it was the need for order – has not been satisfied.

At this point, your interlocutor was worried about something – an uncomfortable feeling. Feelings come from met or unmet human needs. You can safely guess that meeting needs leads to pleasant feelings whereas not meeting needs leads to uncomfortable ones.

Feelings run fast and trigger reactions that people do not consciously control. First, there is an emotion, which is a mental process that causes physiological reactions in the body such as a burst of hormones or a muscle spasm. From the point of view of evolution, the part of brain responsible for transmitting commands in response to emotional stimulus is ancient. It is responsible for the basic reactions associated with survival: fight or flight. It must therefore act very quickly.

There is however a simple method for delaying your emotional response after the appearance of a stimulus, which boils down to realizing your emotions: to gain some time, you have to pass the information about the emotional reaction, which travels from your brain to the rest of the body, through a slightly longer path. The easiest way to do it is to engage your brain's abstract thinking and speech areas. Both of these areas are located in the cerebral cortex, which developed later in our evolution and which acts more slowly than the central brain that's responsible for emotions.

So what do you have to do? Name the emotion you are feeling, which uses abstract thinking, and say it out loud, which obviously uses the speech area. To help you prepare to do this, table 9.2 presents a list of names of feelings – it's nice to have more than "good" or "not good" on hand to describe an emotion.

• Bliss	• Wonder	• Anger
• Pleasure	• Inspiration	• Irritation
• Relaxation	• Being intrigued	• Concern
• Movement	• Curiosity	• Indifference
• Amusement	• Excitement	• Heaviness
• Tenderness	• Pride	• Powerlessness
• Exhilaration	• Passivity	• Sleepiness
• Focus	• Pain	• Frustration
• Fulfillment	• Reluctance	• Tension
• Freedom	• Anxiety	• Being overwhelmed
• Elevation	• Discomfort	• Feeling down
• Captivation	• Fury	• Indecision
• Sensitivity	• Uncertainty	• Regret
• Delight	• Distrust	• Astonishment
• Surprise	• Depression	

Table 9.2. Feelings in NVC, after Rosenberg.

Perhaps you've concluded that an interlocutor who shouts "You're pissing me off!" is in fact naming the feeling of anger. Nothing could be further from the truth! There is a huge difference between "You're pissing me off!" and "I feel pissed off."

In the first statement, the interlocutor makes you responsible for those feelings. But this specific feeling is only the result of unmet needs. "You're pissing me off!" does not name feelings but throws an accusation. Only the following statements would truly describe feelings:

• I feel anger!

• I feel happiness!

• I feel frustration!

• I feel moved!

On the other hand, the interlocutor could also say:

• I feel that you don't understand me!

• I feel trapped!

• I feel that I am going mad!

These are statements taken from ordinary language – people talk this way. These last three statements do not describe feelings; these are evaluations in disguise. They evaluate, respectively, the interlocutor ("YOU do not understand me"), the situation ("trapped"), and future action ("going mad"). NVC calls such expressions a "sense". They are not named emotional states but emotionally coloured utterances, in which someone simply used the verb "feel".

The communication model in NVC

"You're pissing me off!"

Let's recap what you know…. You now know that your interlocutor saw that you came to the meeting five minutes after the appointed time or heard that you called his/her idea pointless. You know that the exclamation means that the interlocutor's need for order has not been satisfied.

Anger, frustration, or grief made the interlocutor shout, "You're pissing me off!"

NVC offers a model of communication that accounts for all the stages of the process described above and provides a process by which to maintain contact with the interlocutor and possibly to ask him/her to change his/her behaviour. The model looks like this:

1. When I/you see/hear <observation>,
2. I/you feel <feeling>
3. because I/you need <need>,
4. so could you <request for a change in behaviour>, please?

This pattern illustrates versions of the NVC in cases when:

- my needs are not met and therefore I experience unpleasant feelings and want to ask someone to change their behaviour; and
- I see signs of unpleasant feelings in my interlocutor so I try to name these feelings and the needs behind them, and then I suggest some action on my part.

Analyze the conversation in table 9.3 to observe the effect of this model in practice

Client	Specialist	Comment
"Why is there no error message?"	-	-
-	"We just wanted to show the idea. We'll add some nice screens during the week."	-
"But I can't show this. You know what? Every time you show me something, it has shortcomings. You're really pissing me off!"	-	The client expresses his/her feelings and, in doing so, calls the results of the work "shortcomings". This makes the professionals responsible for the clients own feelings of "pissing me off".
-	"When you say that we're pissing you off, do you feel angry because you need to be certain?"	First, understand the needs of the interlocutor then express your needs. Respecting the guidelines above, the specialist uses the NVC model. He is trying to guess the need. Maybe this is all about certainty? Please note that the specialist is focused on talking about the observation ("you say that we're pissing you off") and does not confuse the observation with evaluations such as "when you accuse us" or "when you're picking on us".
"Yes! I'm angry!"	-	It appears that the specialist correctly identified the client's feeling. The client does not refer directly to the need. This confirms that there is a positive intention behind the unpleasant feeling.
-	"And you'd prefer that our solutions are ready for you to show them to the client?"	This leads to the next step, which is the suggestion of a change in the specialist's behaviour.

"Well, that's my point."	-	The client acknowledges that, yes, he/she expects such a change in behavior.
-	"I understand. You know, when you call our screens 'shortcomings', I feel sad because I need recognition. Maybe next time you could simply say that you do not accept the work and we will simply correct it?	This is the moment the specialist talks about his/her own needs and feelings, and then asks the client to change behavior.
"I will think about it."	-	Because the client's needs have been recognized, he/she is also willing to recognize the needs of the specialist.

Table 8.3. The NVC model in practice.

If you're thinking that NVC seems strange or artificial and you're wondering why on earth you should speak this way, read the following paragraphs. This is necessary!

Do I have to speak so oddly?

No, you do not have to. You should not, even, because using the NVC model in a literal way is surprising for the majority of people and eventually makes them angry. Why? This is more or less the same as code retreat and writing code without using the "if" statement. In your daily work, you might not use it, but when you avoid ifs, you learn to use polymorphism. In *Nonviolent Communication: A Language of Life*[1] (2003), Rosenberg states:

> The NVC is only a model. You train it to internalize it. This is it! Practice talking with the NVC model to internalize it in your thinking, in your processing, and in the way you analyze messages produced by your interlocutors. The model will help you sort out what you hear.

> You need to know exactly what your interlocutor produces, what is an observation, what is an evaluation, and what is a need. The model is designed to accurately decompose imprecise and emotional messages, and then to react accordingly to establish contact with the interlocutor.

> Keep the model in mind, but do not write it out loud.

---

1   https://www.amazon.com/Nonviolent-Communication-Language-Marshall-Rosenberg/dp/1892005034?ie=UTF8&*Version*=1&*entries*=0

You might ask what to say if you're not meant to write it out loud. According to the NVC model, you analyze what your interlocutor says and does, and in the course of the conversation you precisely refer to feelings, needs, and observations using what some people call the "street NVC". Analyze the conversation in table 8.4.

Client	Specialist	Comment
"Why is there no error message?"	-	-
-	"We just wanted to show the idea. We'll add some nice screens during the week."	-
"But I can't show this. You know what? Every time you show me something, it has shortcomings. You're really pissing me off!"	-	The client expresses his/her feelings and, in doing so, calls the results of the work "shortcomings". This makes the professionals responsible for the clients own feelings of "pissing me off".
-	"I don't know what to say. You must be really angry."	The specialist heard the message "you're really pissing me off" then thought about it according to the NVC model and identified the feeling behind this message: anger. Only then did the specialist name it aloud.
"How should I feel if we still can't figure out our co-operation!?"	-	The client acknowledges it. Remember that feelings are not mathematics. The client's confirmation does not mean "Yes, according to the ISO335-11 specification, this is 'anger'"; rather, this is something like "Hmm, yes, the word 'anger' roughly fits what I'm feeling."
-	"Well, my guess is that you'd prefer to work in better conditions. After all, trusting the team is important."	The specialist is trying to name the human need, which in this situation has not been satisfied. The specialist chooses "trust".

Client	Specialist	Comment
"Indeed. And I already do not trust you."	-	That was a good choice. Trust is roughly what the client has on his mind.
		The client has confirmed it, but is still saying something about the professional: "I do not trust you." Note that the client has consciously or unconsciously directly named his need: he lacks trust.
-	"Because you're concerned that you'll get a shortcoming again?"	Since the client has named the need, the specialist is trying to name the feeling associated with this need being unmet. He decides on "concern".
		Then the specialist wants to identify the event that caused the client to feel concerned. Again, here the specialist links the need (concern) with the observation ("you'll get a shortcoming again").
		The specialist did use the word "shortcoming", which is more of an evaluation than an observation, but did it consciously to simplify the communication after conducting an internal analysis according to the NVC model. All in all, it was an evaluation invented by the client.
"That's the point."	-	Again, the specialist was correct in naming what the client is experiencing: concern.
		But what happens if you make a mistake in naming the needs or feelings? Nothing, just keep on trying to find the correct one.

Client	Specialist	Comment
-	"I think I see what the problem is. I can suggest something."	The specialist has previously shown empathy to establish good rapport with the client. Now, the specialist smoothly moves to a point where he/she will be able to talk about his/her own perspective and needs.
"Yes?"	-	It turns out that the client is willing to follow the direction of the conversation set by the specialist.
-	"As far as I understand, it's ultimately about delivering a completely ready functionality. It's also very important for us to handle situations when something doesn't go as you expect."	The first sentence is a familiar paraphrase. This way, the specialist once again makes sure that he understood the situation of the interlocutor. Only in the second sentence does the specialist begin to report his/her own needs.
"What do you mean?"	-	The client is in contact with the specialist.
	"For example, when you call what we give you 'shortcomings', it's really frustrating. We're committed to maintaining good relations, so maybe you could pop in more often to have a look at these screens on an ongoing basis?"	The specialist indicates that the behaviour of calling the work "shortcomings" evokes a specific feeling of "frustration" then communicates the need – i.e. "good relations" – and asks for a change of behavior: "you could pop in more often".
"That's a good idea."	-	As you can see, agreement without violence is possible!

Table 8.4. Street NVC in practice.

As you can see, the street version of NVC is completely natural and can be used in every conversation.

Some potential misunderstandings

At a number of IT conferences, especially those with topics related to agile software development, many speakers refer to NVC. Nonetheless, there are several recurrent misunderstandings that I would like to address.

Literal application of the NVC model: Yes, speaking in this specific manner sounds awkward. We have discussed this in detail above.

NVC does not work: This is a frequent objection, expressed, for example as: "I tried to use NVC in a conversation with my boss and it didn't work," "I tried it in the team and it didn't work," or "I tried it with my children and it wasn't working." Usually in such situations, we ask precision questions like "How exactly did you decide that it didn't work?" It often turns out that the person hoped that using NVC would allow him/her to persuade interlocutors to change their mind.

My goodness! This turns a method that focuses on respect for humans and open communication into a tool for forcing interlocutors to change their mind. This is a total perversion of the method. NVC trainers, somewhat perversely as well, call this specific way of thinking "VNC" for "violent non-communication".

The very question "Does NVC work?" is a bit out of place. The objective of NVC is neither to achieve tangible results nor to solve problems during a conversation. The objective of NVC is to eliminate violence from communication, to have you show empathy, and to let you maintain contact with the needs that you and your interlocutors have.

What is empathy?: The best definition has been provided by Rosenberg himself, who said that the longer we train ourselves in the NVC model, the more clearly we realize that behind all the messages that have always sounded scary, simply lie only unmet needs of people who ask us to do something to improve their well-being.

Why use NVC?: If NVC is not about any particular outcome or persuasion, then why should you even bother with it? Well, the sincere answer that comes to my mind is because it is right. It is right to care and talk about your needs – and to have the same attitude towards the needs of others. It is right to speak about your experiences and to listen to the feelings of your interlocutors. Just be in touch, without guilt or coercion. I am convinced by the vision of a world in which people function this way, even if this vision does not come true quickly enough.

www.ingramcontent.com/pod-product-compliance
Lightning Source LLC
Chambersburg PA
CBHW022116170526
45157CB00004B/1673